TRAVELING THROUGH

CELEBRITIES FROM THE 40'S AND 50'S

JEANNE BEATTY

Traveling Through
Celebrities from the 40's and 50's

Dedication

To my daughter, Jeanne Elizabeth Holdal,
who said to me one day, "Mom, you should
write all this down while people who
recognize these names are still alive"

CHAPTERS

PREFACE

This book is a series of reflections of celebrities from a different time. I was a child when I met most of them. It probably is well for all of us to consider that one never knows who may be watching. One never knows whom we may be impressing or not impressing. Often it is children.

Many of you may not recognize some of the names in this book. However, it is worth reading as it will give you a bit of an insight into a time long past and a people, many of whom are long gone.

In reflection, I am led to one very significant conclusion. All generations are fleeting. Those who were "on the top of the world," internationally known, admired, worshipped, and celebrated, have moved into the pages of history. To name a few: Joan Crawford, Clark Gable, Rock Hudson, Bette Davis, William Holden, Shirley Temple, and Bob Hope.

So, it will be with the current generation.

Then, one day in the future, this young and under-forty generation will turn around and find itself celebrating the younger people in the generation coming up behind them. And then they also will be met with blank stares.

That is when you realize that—everyone leaves— eventually.

So, is that not what all of us are doing . . . just *traveling through?*

RUTH HARDY, MEL HABER & INGLESIDE INN

When I was seven years old my parents began visiting Palm Springs, California, every winter for several months. For some reason, they always took me out of school to go with them.

They stayed at a delightful little place; in today's vernacular, it would be called a boutique hotel. It was Ingleside Inn, where the rich and famous stayed.

But no matter how rich or famous a person was, they did not stay there unless they were recommended by at least one former guest.

Ingleside Inn Courtyard
Photo by Steve Kepple – By Permission of PlumpJack Hospitality Group

This was the hard and fast rule of the proprietor, Ruth Hardy, who travelled to the desert in the late 1930's and after purchasing the property, turned it into an Inn.

Most of the guests returned every winter year after year, from the San Francisco Bay area, Los Angeles, the Midwest, and the East Coast. Over time the guests became more like a family.

It was so much a family atmosphere that, one winter when I was ten-years old, Ruth Hardy volunteered to take care of me on several occasions when my parents could not find a sitter.

I gained some insight on what she was all about on those occasions. She was in essence a hotel woman, as if she had been born to it. As a one-person owner/manager of Ingleside Inn, she knew every guest by name, including their preferences. Even though never disclosed by her, she knew some of their problems, so part-time counselor could be added to her list of accomplishments. One thing she did not know, which became obvious to me at a young age, was that she had absolutely no idea about what to do with a ten- year old girl.

Mel Haber purchased Ingleside Inn, Palm Springs in 1975.

I met him on several visits after he became the new owner. And although he is not a celebrity, per se, I included him in this book because he is a part of the ongoing saga of Ingleside Inn and Palm Springs, figuring into it quite naturally.

He impressed me for his charm and graciousness. He was a natural born, hands-on, hotel owner/manager/host.

Mel told me of Ruth's "card file" that she kept on the guests. She rated her guests "Good" and "No Good." He said he found my family in the "Good" stack of cards, not that it really mattered after all that time, but it was rather amusing. I know that none of her guests over the years ever knew of this rating system.

Though Mel had made significant changes, notably the addition of Melvyn's Restaurant, he did maintain the original atmosphere, which was so delightful

Melvyn's Restaurant & Lounge at Ingleside Inn.
Photo by Steve Kepple – By Permission of PlumpJack Hospitality Group

and inviting. It stayed a calm and serene and restful place to relax, enjoy, have fun and unwind and enjoy being with friends.

The biggest surprise on that first visit was the amazing addition of the restaurant, Melvyn's— that fabulous restaurant was eventually featured in "Lives of the Rich and Famous." The food was quality, the dining—elegant.

There is a story (probably true) that if an item was not on the menu, one could order it and it would be served the same day. One guest put that claim to the test and ordered a non-menu item. A plane was dispatched to New York, the only place it was available, and the item was purchased and delivered to the Melvyn's kitchen, then prepared and served to the delight of that very impressed diner. I would not have wanted to get the bill for that meal!

Mel had taken the existing dining room and Ruth's former living quarters, which fronted the service alley between the restaurant and the main building, and developed it into this remarkable restaurant.

The dining room used to be quite simple and had more of a family atmosphere.

There were small tables around the room, which seated two to four people. There was one large round table in the center of the room and a bit off to the side where single people who took their meals. I often thought how lonely those single people, mostly women, seemed.

Music was piped into the dining room every evening from the library in the main building from a stack of pre-selected LP records. One evening a guest, a Stanford student, and friend of mine at the time, was visiting his parents at the Inn. He decided to rearrange the order of the stack of LP records. Most diners, after the initial shock of hearing a classical music selection interrupted by Elvis blaring over the loud speakers, burst out laughing.

Ruth Hardy, the original owner, always made a big deal of her chefs. As in every restaurant, chefs are the celebrities and success is dependent on their artistry. I think she had three in the years she ran the Inn. From time to time she would bring the chef out of the kitchen and introduce him around the room to the accolades of the dinner guests. Keeping a chef happy was the secret of keeping a chef.

Ruth also had a "Girl Friday" who could always be found behind the reception desk. She had her hands on the essential basics of running the Inn, such as registering guests, billing, switchboard (an ancient phone system) and a myriad of other jobs. Mostly she kept things running smoothly.

One visitor in the 1950's, who could be found swimming in the pool every day, but seen nowhere else, was the wife of Krupp, the German industrialist and steel manufacturer. She stayed several days before leaving for Reno for a divorce.

She was tall, blond, elegant, and extremely attractive, and Ruth was concerned that she was driving alone across the desert. She cautioned her, "You better take that 'rock' off your finger and hide it. You are just inviting trouble." It was indeed a diamond of sizable proportion and, I am sure, of flawless quality.

"I am not a bit worried. No one would believe it is real," was her reply.

Virginia's domain was the front desk and the lobby. There was always a large puzzle in the process of completion on a table at the side of the registration desk.

The lobby was also the scene of a nightly cocktail party. Every guest provided their own alcohol, which was labeled with their names and kept in a small kitchen off the library. Ruth often hired a country western singer to entertain at the nightly cocktail hour. He had composed his own rendition of "Home on the Range." His version—"Home, home in Palm Springs where the dear little millionaires play, where seldom is heard an intelligent word, and champagne flows like water all day."

The only time Ingleside Inn provided alcohol was when Ruth honored her pledge. She guaranteed that she would serve her guests champagne any day the sun did not shine in Palm Springs. There were usually around 30 guests at any one time.

It did happen once when I was there. And one time it *almost* happened. Guests awoke to grey skies and the sun did not appear for the rest of the day. Some of them approached Ruth toward evening

saying they were looking forward to champagne being served at the cocktail hour. She told them that
the sun had appeared briefly, at dawn, as reported
by the gardener, Sam, to everyone's disappointment.

Ruth was quite fearless. One morning we learned
at breakfast of her encounter in the middle of the
night with criminals, which she captured without as-
sistance. They had broken into the hotel looking for
cash or whatever else they could steal. Perhaps they
had planned to invade the guest rooms as well when
they were interrupted.

Ruth called the police first, then "captured" them,
using a rolling pin, if I remember correctly, anyway
it was some remote, non-lethal weapon, and herded
them into the dining room where they waited together for the police to arrive.

No one could figure out how one diminutive
woman, she was only about 5'4", could hold two
young men, in great physical shape, by herself until
the police arrived. It was an indication of the power
and authority of her unique personality.

She was also on the City Council for many years.
It was her brilliant idea to put lights on the palm
trees. There is a statue of Ruth Hardy on Palm Canyon Drive commemorating her many contributions
to the city.

That was life at Ingleside Inn in the 1940's and
1950's, where the cares and concerns of the world
were temporarily shut out. Golf, initially played at
O'Donnell Golf Course in the 1940's, was the only

course in the area at the time. Hard to imagine that now. The order of the day at Ingleside Inn was swimming, sunbathing, reading, relaxing by the pool, playing croquet on the "Fields of Hardy," evening cocktails, and fine dining.

An annual croquet tournament was held every year on the Field of Hardy. Teams were auctioned off the night before. The proceeds were donated to the Red Cross, which usually amounted to $20,000, a tidy sum in the 1950's.

I have not been back to Ingleside Inn for many years but before closing this chapter I have fond memories of a tradition that was "set in cement".

There I was at age 9, diving off the board at Ingleside Inn pool.

Whenever a guest was leaving, driving away after a visit, Ruth would always appear and ring the large bell that was hanging on the veranda near the entrance to the lobby. This tradition assured the guest(s) would return.

Only once, in the many years I stayed there, did Ruth not show up to ring the bell. Those people must have been in the stack "No Good" guest cards.

Ingleside's pool area - a perfect place to relax.
Photo by Steve Kepple – Permission of PlumpJack Hospitality Group

ALFRED "WALLY" WALLENSTEIN

Alfred ("Wally") Wallenstein, the celebrated cellist and a director of the Los Angeles Philharmonic at the time, was a guest of Ingleside Inn in the 1950's.

He was one of the most unassuming people that I have ever met, considering his enormous talent.

He and his wife had no children, and perhaps that is why he sort of took me "under his wing." I spent hours playing croquet with him on the "Fields of Hardy."

I should explain that the way croquet was played there was *not* a child's game. A professional croquet set, ordered from England, was used. An annual auction was held, where people "purchased" players, as mentioned above, the night before the annual tournament.

The proceeds that were raised for the tournament, usually around $20,000, went to the Red Cross. I was fortunate to win the singles trophy one year, although I was only fourteen at the time.

Wally was kind, most gracious, easy to know, fun to be around, and a terrific croquet player. When he wasn't wielding his conductor's baton, he did quite well wielding a croquet mallet.

LILY PONS

She was a tiny bundle of dynamite with a voice to match.

Lily Pons was one of the most celebrated coloratura opera singers of her time.

She stayed at Ingleside Inn, where I got to know her, until she built a home in the desert.

I can see her still as she swept through the gardens and lobby. She was a dramatic sweeper. She seemed super-charged, like she had an extra battery tucked away inside.

She would often bring her miniature poodle with her that was dyed to match the color outfit she was wearing.

Flamboyant is the word I would use to describe her. She was also very open, transparent and friendly.

My mother and I were invited to the home she had built in Palm Springs soon after it was finished.

We were served tea on a tray with one of André Kostelanetz' own arrangements of orchestral music under the glass. He was a popular conductor of "easy listening" music from classical to Broadway show tunes, which reached sales of over 50 million.

There were also dozens of other mementos around the house and pool area in remembrance of her career and the many famous people she called her friends. It was a memorable and delightful after-noon. Regrettably, she did not sing for us.

SANTOS
A "SPREADING" SUCCESS

Santos was not a celebrity by how the world defines a celebrity. He was probably not known to many people outside of the Palm Springs area. He was, however, a celebrity and a success in his own right.

Santos was a waiter at the Tennis Club in Palm Springs in the 1940's. He came from the Philippines and settled in California. He was charming, gregarious and liked by everyone.

During his career at the Tennis Club he developed a cheese spread that at that time was unusual, unique and extremely delicious. He called it "Santos Spread."

The Tennis Club served it and in time he bottled it and sold it at a deli on Palm Canyon Drive. They soon found that they had trouble keeping it in stock as it sold out almost as quickly as it came in.

From this small beginning Santos eventually opened his own restaurant in Palm Springs, which became a favorite place to eat for the locals and the tourists alike. Though many people pleaded and begged him for his recipe he never gave it up. Some tried on their own to duplicate it but fell short of the unique flavor and consistency.

Santos, his cheese spread, and eventually his successful restaurant are part of Palm Springs legend now, so in his own unique way could be called a celebrity.

BOB HOPE

I did not know him well, but I did meet him several times and saw him on stage once.

I saw him on stage, at the Plaza Theatre in Palm Springs, in 1949. It was the first time I saw him perform in person along with Les Brown and his Band of Renown. In several years they would be going off to entertain the troops together in South Korea. He tossed out the jokes so fast one had to scramble to catch up.

Bob Hope, in fine form.

He was entertaining even when he was not on stage. One evening, about a year later, I was traveling with my family on the Southern Pacific train from Palm Springs to Los Angeles. We were sitting across from him in the dining car and he was reading the menu when the waiter came to his table to take his order. "Diplomat soup," he said, reading from the menu. "Does that mean I need to be a diplomat to eat it?" Obviously, his writers were not with him on that trip but he couldn't seem to stop himself from joking around, even about soup!

Another time, perhaps four or five years later, he was seated with his family, at a restaurant in Palm Springs. I was so impressed watching him interact with his children, as if they were the only people in the world. I think the catch phrase today is "quality time" but he was not in need of instruction of child/parent relationships, it seemed to me that he had that one down pat.

The last time I saw Bob Hope was the morning he was being driven down University Avenue in Palo Alto in a long, black limousine, and with the windows down, he was waving to the gathering crowd along the route. He was on his way to attend the 1985 Super Bowl between the San Francisco 49ers and the Miami Dolphins, which was being played that year at Stanford Stadium.

I had brunch that morning at a local restaurant in town, not realizing that it would be packed with cheering Miami Dolphin fans. They were actually celebrating their victory before the game began. I imagine the trip back home was a lot quieter.

The final score was 49ers 38, Dolphins 16.

Overall, in those few brief encounters with Bob Hope I would say that my impression of him was that of a man who truly enjoyed life, lived it to the full, and seemed as comfortable with himself as the wearing of old shoes.

DOLORES HOPE

Bob Hope's wife was rarely in front of a camera or in the limelight. Most of his fans probably never saw her.

She had a beautiful voice and a successful singing career during the big band era of the 1930's and 1940's.

I met her several times as she was shopping at Bullock's on Palm Canyon Drive. During that time there were two major stores on Palm Canyon Drive, which were across the street from each other.

And off topic for a moment, I must mention Louise's Pantry next to the Plaza Theatre. It was a popular restaurant for many decades, and the line of customers for breakfast would extend down the street. They served the most delicious French Toast I have ever tasted – then or since.

Getting back to my impression of Dolores Hope, she was rather regal, very elegant, soft-spoken and a lady through-and-through. One of the most charming, delightful, and genuine people I met at that time.

LUCILLE BALL

She was a glamour girl with all the trappings of a Hollywood star.

I saw her and spoke with her several times while we were shopping (not together) at Bullock's.

She and her husband opened the Indian Wells Resort as an investment in 1957. It was spectacular and innovative for the time.

I was a teenager then and one of the thousands of fans who watched "I Love Lucy" faithfully every week.

She had great timing, humor, and stage presence, even off the stage.

Lucille Ball and Desi Arnaz

But looking back and remembering her now, I recognize something about her that I was too young to notice then. There was an underlying sadness about her.

Later it became evident that her marriage was not a happy one, and it ended eventually in divorce.

NORMAN VINCENT PEALE

He was the author of the book, "The Power of Positive Thinking," which became the number-one best-seller in the 1950's. It was around 1958 when he traveled to Palm Springs with a staff member who was active in his church in New York, Marble Collegiate Church, working there as a counselor. They had travelled to the desert to be with Lucille Ball at the time her marriage was breaking up.

When we met, he told me I would be most successful in the hotel industry. At that time, I was managing a hotel in Palm Springs that my parents bought as an investment. I must have learned something from the years of observing Ruth Hardy in action. I did not follow his advice; and after a year in the hotel business, I returned to college.

He was, it seemed to me anyway, very much of a corporate, president type. That was my impression, al-though he was there in the capacity of a pastor.

JOAN CRAWFORD

I met her at the Chi Chi Club in Palm Spring when I was ten years-old while dining there with my parents.

With their permission, I gathered up my courage and went over to her table where she was having dinner with some friends. I did not recognize any of them but they were no doubt also Hollywood movie stars. They just looked old to me. But not Joan Crawford, she looked lovely, radiant and larger than life.

The minute she spoke to me all my shyness vanished. She was gracious, and charming and seemed interested in me.

Years later, when I read the book her daughter wrote about her, "Mommy Dearest," it did not seem possible that it was the same person. I thought, however, if that book was true, I

Joan Crawford – fan friendly.

was most grateful to have been one of her fans and not one of her children.

CHARLES FARRELL

harlie Farrell, owner of The Racquet Club in Palm Springs, and co-star with Janet Gaynor in the movie, *Seventh Heaven*, was where the movie crowd hung out until a lot of them started building their own houses and even golf and country clubs in Palm Desert. Until then the desert outside of Palm Springs was just a wide, open-spaced sandbox with, as the song says, tumbling tumbleweeds.

Charles Farrell

During that time, before the houses, golf courses, and country clubs there was a great place to horseback ride in Palm Desert called the Smoke Tree Ranch. I never saw anyone famous there although I knew that some movie people liked to go there. I think I was too busy galloping as fast as I could across the wide-open spaces.

Charlie Farrell was always "on call." He was the host supreme who catered to his guests with charm, wit, aplomb, and humor.

It was there that one would see loads of celebrities in the 1940's and part of the 1950's.

One could see a lot of good tennis played there. However, one never saw anyone swim in the lovely, large, and very inviting swimming pool. It was not *de rigueur* or just not done. As a child I thought this to be a terrible waste. I asked once, "Why doesn't anyone swim there?" "Because," the answer was, "If they ever did everyone would know that they did not *belong* and they would probably be mocked and ridiculed. That, I thought, was most likely worse than possibly drowning.

There was another private club in Palm Springs, The Tennis Club, which was near Ingleside Inn. But it had a completely different atmosphere. It was celebrated for its exquisite and unique dining room with a dance floor that was built into the side of a mountain. From time to time one would see champion tennis players on the courts such as Jack Kramer, 1947 Wimbledon champion and Pancho Gonzales, known as the greatest server of all time and who won the United States titles back to back in 1948 and 1949.

I did watch Jack Kramer playing tennis there one day, but unfortunately, I was only nine years old and did not pick up a racquet for another year. Looking back, I do wish I had been old enough and known enough to appreciate the privilege of watching him play.

DINAH SHORE &
KIRK DOUGLAS

I only mention them together because that is where I saw them – playing tennis *together* – at the Racquet Club. I watched them play singles for hours. I was a few years older then, in my teens, and appreciated the game, played the game, and knew the lingo and the rules.

I used to sit on the sidelines and admire them because, number one, they were stars and I was an impressionable teenager, and two, because they were dynamic on the court with great rhythm, timing, terrific to watch with their seemingly boundless and unlimited energy and fantastic concentration.

I used to fantasize that they would ask me to join them at least once. They never did. It must have been that incredible concentration they had on the court. I think most likely they never even saw me sitting there.

ROCK HUDSON

He was a guest at the Racquet Club in Palm Springs along with dozens of other Hollywood legends before many of them began building homes in Palm Desert in the 1950's.

I saw him once soon after the movie *The Giant* was released. A smash hit in 1956 that he stared in with Elizabeth Taylor.

He was hard to miss.

When he walked into the dining room of the Racquet Club one evening all motion, all conversation, all eating and drinking, came to a dead stop. It was as if someone pulled a plug and all the air left the room.

Rock Hudson – the essence of celebrity in the 1950's.

Everyone stared, transfixed at this incredibly tall, 6' 6", and exceptionally handsome man. The room got so quiet that one could hear a whisper.

He just stood at the entrance for a bit which made even more of an impression and I am sure he was aware of the reaction he received, but somehow, I thought at the time, he was embarrassed by the attention, as if he never got quite used to it. When he found the people and the table he was looking for and moved on, life in the dining room resumed its normal pace again.

WILLIAM POWELL

I met him one evening at the Racquet Club in Palm Springs. He was most well-known for the title role in the "Thin Man" movie series. He was having dinner there with his wife, Mousie (her nickname) and friends.

He was charisma itself.

If one would take his features and analyze them one by one, he was not very good looking. But his sophisticated, *bon vivant* charm and graciousness made him a very appealing and romantic figure.

GEORGE BURNS &
GRACIE ALLEN

This is another couple that is better represented together.

I met them very early on, around 1949 in Palm Springs at the first health-food store to open there.

I was quite young then and shopping with my mother, who was a health food junkie.

As I reflect on how they appeared to me, I would say that they had a most remarkable and loving relationship. It was clear for anyone to see even when they were just shopping.

It was obvious in seeing them together how totally dedicated George Burns was to his wife. It was as if she was the only person in the world.

How very difficult it must have been for him when he lost her so young and lived all the ensuing years alone.

He lived to be 100 years old.

He most likely kept shopping at health food stores.

WILLIAM HOLDEN

I didn't so much meet him, as he crashed into me while I was on the dance floor at the Racquet Club in Palm Springs. He was rushing across the dance floor toward the cabanas off the swimming pool and he seemed to be in a dreadful rush.

I was celebrating my 21st birthday, enjoying dinner and dancing with a friend.

William Holden – May I have this dance?

And what could be a better birthday present than to meet this Hollywood celebrity—and so close up and personal.

If only I had been a bit older or perhaps a bit bolder, the encounter might have been even more thrilling than it was.

Suffice to say, I was totally tongue-tied and went weak in the knees, I think my date had to hold me upright.

In retrospect, if I had maintained my equilibrium and presence of mind at the time I would have said,

"You nearly knocked me down and I am here celebrating my 21st birthday, that is going to cost you one dance."

I wonder how he would have responded. I will never know. But I like to think that we would have had that dance.

DAVID NIVEN, CLARK GABLE & ALAN LADD

David Niven, Clark Gable, and Alan Ladd were three of the most popular stars in Hollywood at that time and the heartthrobs of millions of women, and teenagers, myself, included.

The first two celebrities are only mentioned together here because I saw them, actually stood next to them – speechless – in the same week.

I stood next to David Niven in front of Bullocks on Palm Canyon Drive waiting for the traffic light to change. He crossed the street but strangely I found myself still standing there, starring after him, as the light turned red again, perhaps several times. I stood right next to Clark Gable in line at Nate's Deli. I think it was the best

Clark Gable – known as the "King of Hollywood."

deli outside of New York City. Their corned beef sandwiches were out of this world. Most of the rich

41

and famous thought so too, because you could see them there quite often at lunchtime. There we stood, Clark Gable, and me, side by side in the order line, and this found me, once again, speechless. After he ordered, I walked up to give my order. That was a most unforgettable corned beef sandwich ever.

A few years later Alan Ladd opened a hardware store in Palm Springs in the early 1950's. I think that most of the women and girls who went there did not go to shop for hammers, nails, tools and building materials but to meet Alan Ladd. I went to his store several times hoping to see him there but all I ever saw was a litter of kittens that decided to be born there soon after the store opened.

WILLIAM BOYD
("HOPALONG CASSIDY")

William Boyd, better known as Hopalong Cassidy.

He starred in a TV series from 1952-1954, as a western cowboy hero. He was always dressed in black wearing a large, black cowboy hat and riding a pure white horse. He was so popular that he appeared on the cover of one issue of *Life* Magazine.

He was one of the first celebrities to build a house in Palm Desert in the 1950's. People would drive out, making a special trip, to see it because it was so very unique.

The house and grounds were entirely black and white. He accomplished this dramatic effect by covering the ground in the front of the house with black and white stones. Ranch houses were beginning to become popular at the time, his was one of the first on the desert, and the use of stones was unique and quite a novelty at that time.

I never saw him, or his horse, anywhere in Palm Springs or Palm Desert, for that matter. But I was impressed with his house, which carried out his TV series color scheme, making a statement that was hard to miss.

PRESIDENT "IKE" EISENHOWER

A lthough this is not my story, it relates several humorous incidents that happened to a member of my family.

President Eisenhower was a Five Star General, whom the public referred to as Ike. So much so that when he was running for his first term for President in 1952, bumper stickers appeared everywhere with the slogan, "I like Ike." One guest at Ingleside Inn put a bumper sticker that read,

Eisenhower campaign button.

"Ike likes me", on his Rolls Royce. It was soon removed when other guests suggested that it might convey the wrong message to a lot of people. Such as Ike is especially partial to those who can afford to drive a Rolls Royce.

He could be found often in Palm Desert playing golf, more so after his eight years in office.

On one occasion, when he was visiting Palm Springs, and everyone always knew when he was there, my parents were shopping with another couple at Bullocks.

The husbands left the store, being bored as most husbands are with the vagaries of shopping and the time it takes for most wives to accomplish it.

They were standing outside the store when a group of people, maybe seven or eight, rushed up to them and requested, "Mr. President, can we have your autograph?" I should explain that my dad looked so much like Eisenhower he could have been his twin brother.

At that time, my mother and her friend were exiting Bullocks when the man who was with my dad rushed them back inside, much to their surprise, exclaiming, "Get back inside. Neither one of you looks like 'Mamie' [Ike's wife]."

Evidentially, my dad signed his own name, and no one seemed to notice at the time. I am sure that they wondered about it later on, when they looked at the autographs more closely.

Another incident occurred several years later at the Bohemian Grove in northern California. My dad went there for two weeks every summer, as did most of the members of the Bohemian Club in San Francisco.

One particular summer, Eisenhower was a guest there. My dad was strolling back with several friends from Skeet shooting when several men along the path stopped them and asked my dad for his autograph. He had once again been mistaken for Eisenhower and it was assumed, wrongly, that the men on either side of him were Secret Service. "He doesn't sign on vacation," one of the guys piped up and so everyone went on their way.

SNIFFS DATE FARM

Another celebrated place my parents visited every year was Sniffs Date Farm, which is popular to this day.

It is located in Indio, 23 miles from Palm Springs. At that time, in the 1940's and early 1950's it seemed more like 100 miles as we drove through mile after mile of desert sand and sagebrush and tumbling tumbleweeds.

On arriving we toured the farm and listened to the lecture on dates. It was more than I ever wanted to know. I remember how ludicrous it seemed, at least from a child's point of view, to emphasize the sexual proclivities of dates both in the lecture and written about in their brochures. They did not need the smarts of Madison Avenue to teach them that sex sells—date trees being no exception.

After the tour my parents would purchase boxes of dates to send to friends back home as well as some for themselves. I never liked the taste or texture but there was another store in Palm Springs that was my kind of store. Fun in the Sun Candies featured marshmallows covered in chocolate, caramel, and strawberry fondant. They began selling these absolutely delicious treats at a folding table set up in front of the Plaza Theatre on Palm Canyon Drive and within several years opened a store at the north end of town.

LORETTA YOUNG

She was one of the few movie stars I did not meet in Palm Springs. She was staying, as was my family, for a week at the Ojai Valley Inn, Ojai, California.

We were having dinner one evening and she sat near us in the dining room with her family. When it looked like she was about to leave, I summoned up my twelve-year old courage and got up and went over to her table to talk with her.

I soon forgot I was ever nervous. She was absolutely charming and so gracious that she put me at ease immediately just as Joan Crawford had done. Years later a friend told me that the Hollywood studios taught their stars how to project their "public image."

She mentioned that she had enjoyed watching me diving earlier that day and thought I should train for the Olympics. That sort of blew me away, figuratively, out of the water. She promised she would come by the next day to watch me again. It didn't happen. I found out later that she had to leave early to return home.

Anyway, it was a thrill.

Did I ever try out for the Olympics? The coach who I worked with at the time thought I should. But my mother, who was afraid of the water and did not swim was, as you can imagine, terrified of me going off the high board.

End of an *almost* gold medal.

THE ROYAL HAWAIIAN HOTEL

M any celebrities were guests at the Royal Hawaiian Hotel after WW2 in the late1940's and beyond.

The Royal Hawaiian Hotel, also known as the Pink Palace, is a "celebrity" in its own right. It is an elegant, charming structure that somehow, just by looking at it, seems to impart the invitation, "Come

The front of the Royal Hawaiian Hotel – the "pink palace."
Photo by permission of Creative Commons

and experience all the delights the Island has to offer; flowers, fragrance, food, sandy beach, surf, comfortable and exquisite accommodations and hospitality at its finest." These amenities have continued through the decades.

Only DC-3s flew from San Francisco and Los Angeles in 1947. It was a sixteen-hour flight

back then. That year was my first encounter with the other side of the Pacific Ocean; with the trade winds, the tropical paradise, and the vibrant shifting

51

blues of the water, the delicious taste of mangoes and papayas, the coconut palms, and the fragrance of the flowers that grew everywhere. What better fragrance is there in the entire world than that of plumeria blossoms? The beauty and wonder of this tropical island seized my heart immediately, never to leave.

At that time, the only three hotels on Waikiki were The Royal Hawaiian, The Halekulani and the Moana. There was a fierce completion to attract tourists to the Islands at the end of the war so there were often perks. On our first visit in 1947, the Royal Hawaiian offered an amazing gesture in the way of Hawaiian hospitality. I remember that courtesy to this day, and my parents were so impressed that they returned to stay many times and recommended the hotel to their friends on the mainland.

+ + +

Now, let me digress a bit and say a few words about Maui in 1947.

We were scheduled to visit Maui and stay at the Hana Maui Hotel for a week. The management of the Royal Hawaiian told us to leave our luggage in the suite for a week or longer if needed at no extra charge. Wow. Imagine that ever happening anywhere in this era of intense tourism.

Maui was getting its first taste of tourism in 1947. We flew from Oahu to Maui on a 12-passenger, single-engine prop plane and landed in a cleared-out sugarcane field. It was enough of a bumpy landing to scare the socks off several passengers. The delight of every guest at the hotel was the banana bread, baked fresh daily. What is common place now was unique then. We coaxed the recipe out of the chef. What gave the bread its unique taste was the addition of buttermilk. The Hana Maui Hotel, now called the Travaasa Hana, is a slice of paradise within paradise.

+ + +

Now, back to The Royal on Oahu.

The Royal also hosted a pineapple juice bar in the lobby for its guests. A lovely and generous touch and appreciated by everyone—including non-guests. Word soon got around and people would wander in off Kalakaua Avenue, for a refresher.

In 1947 and for several years after, the open air and Hawaiian theme restaurant was unique in the individual service it offered. A hostess was assigned to each table for the duration of the each guest's stay. I cannot remember the name of our hostess but she was a delightful, lovely, young Hawaiian woman, about nineteen years old. We became good friends, since she was not only a hostess in the dining room but became my companion during the day while my parents had "their" vacation. She expanded my education and love for the Islands and the Hawaiian people and also taught me the hula, which I continued to study on each subsequent visit.

At that time, The Royal Hawaiian had extensive gardens and Kalakaua had native bamboo stalls along the avenue selling the heavenly fragrant leis. Needless to say there was not a high rise in sight. The Waikiki area seemed like a native village compared to today, and Kalakaua Avenue became known as the Champs-Elysees of Oahu.

Several of the Hollywood stars that I remember for their "performances" at the hotel were Bette Davis and Burt Lancaster. He was staying there during the filming "From Here to Eternity."

I was swimming and sunning and enjoying a day on the beach and watching the calisthenics and cartwheels that Burt Lancaster was performing. He was actually very good.

Suddenly this voice came out of nowhere. Everyone looked up. She was calling to Burt from the terrace of the Royal Hawaiian down to the beach, which was a considerable distance. She did not need a mic. That well-recognized, crackling voice was unmistakably Bette Davis.

There I was, standing in the Hotel's garden.

I am certain that she could have been heard "Beyond the Reef".

THE DUKE

Duke Kahanamoku held "Court" every day, for years, in front of the Royal Hawaiian Hotel on the island of Oahu. It was his turf, his domain and where he had an array of surfboards lined up for rental and lessons.

That is where I first met him when I was ten years old and where he gave me my first surfboard lesson. By the age of twelve, I was surfing tandem.

The Duke was a five-time Olympic medalist in swimming.

Duke and his longboard.

It was about that time that I also first learned to do the Hula, which I pursued for many years.

I met him years later when visiting Oahu at a large reception honoring Mayor Blaisdell, who served as mayor of Honolulu HI from 1955 to 1969. He was the last Republican Mayor to date. It was there that The Duke asked me to do the Hula and said, "You are the only *haole* that does the hula like a native."

The Duke was one terrific guy. He was so loved by everyone who knew him.

*Surfing with a family friend (1951) at Waikiki,
proving that while I was not one of the Duke's
skilled pupils, I could remain standing.*

ROBERT WAGNER &
NATALIE WOOD

I met another famous and adored Hollywood couple at the Mauna Kea Hotel, Hawaii, in 1964.

I was having dinner with my husband and we stopped by their table on our way out to chat.

Robert Wagner and Natalie Wood were most gracious, even though we interrupted their dinner, and they did not seem to mind. We shared experiences of our time in Hawaii that year and we talked about Bing Crosby and his wife who had recently moved to our town of Hillsborough, California.

She was stunning and that evening she wore the most gorgeous ivory bracelets I had ever seen. Years later I read that she always wore bracelets to cover up her wrist. She had an accident when she was quite young that left her with a bone protrusion on her wrist.

They seemed happy together, more than that, it was as though they were natural together, belonged together, and they were made for each other. It was a shock to millions of fans when she died in such a terrible way. Now years later it appears that the boating accident is still a mystery, as was perhaps their relationship.

ANNE BAXTER &
JOHN HODIAK

Anne Baxter was a friend of my parents and visited our home several times in the 1940's and 1950's.

She was married to the actor John Hodiak, who was a golfing buddy of my Dad's whenever he visited the San Francisco Bay Area.

The Hodiaks were divorced in the 1950's and he died very early at the age of 41. He was close to reaching the top of a very promising career as a Hollywood leading man, and so it seemed doubly sad that his life was cut short. He was gracious and unassuming and interested in others more than in himself, which is rather unique for a film "star".

The first time I met Anne, I was about eleven years old. She was "Number One Box Office" then and we sat together at the head table at the Father/Daughter Rotary luncheon at the Palace Hotel in San Francisco.

Anne Baxter

She came to a dinner party in her honor at our house a few years later. I remember playing a party game she taught us that evening. It was all the rage that year in Hollywood. The game is one that cannot be explained, only shown on paper. What was different about it is that it showed their priorities in life were different. Mine turned out to be undecided, probably because I was just fourteen years old at the time.

She had a huge, larger-than-life, dramatic flair, al-though she was quite diminutive in stature. I remember her deep, throaty voice, as if she had smoked too many cigarettes that day.

She was then the number one female star in Hollywood after winning an Academy Award for her role in *All About Eve*. She was about to be given the Number One dressing room at her Studio. Unfortunately, for her, and she felt the sting deeply, another actress appeared on the scene and she was given the Number One dressing room instead. Her name was Marilyn Monroe.

I was with her one last time when I went to tea at her home and met her infant daughter. That time the "actress" disappeared, and she was relaxed and enjoying her new "role" of being a mother.

Later she re-married and moved to Australia.

Anne was the granddaughter of the brilliant architect, Frank Lloyd Wright.

WINNIE MAE, WILL ROGERS & WILEY POST

Wiley Post and Will Rodgers were close friends. Will Rogers, the humorist and stand-up comedian, popular in the 1930's. He is credited with many famous quips, such as when he observed, "I belong to no organized party, I am a Democrat," and "Everything is changing in America. People are taking their comedians seriously and their politicians as a joke."

Winnie Mae, daughter of the famous aviator Wiley Post, was a guest at our home whenever she was in the area.

What stands out from one of her visits was her reaction to a flight she was scheduled to take to Hawaii the following day, August 15th. Later in the day, I learned why she was upset. She was remembering that it was the date of the fatal plane crash that killed her father along with the humorist, Will Rogers. *The Winnie Mae*, the plane named after Wiley Post's daughter, crashed on takeoff near Point Barrow, Alaska.

Wiley Post was the first person to fly around the world solo in July 1933 in a seven-day, 19-hour flight.

She cancelled her flight to Hawaii that afternoon.

*A family friend surrounded by fragrant gardenias.
It was the second BBQ in which my parents floated
5,000 gardenias in our swimming pool.*

SHIRLEY TEMPLE

I met Shirley on the sound stage of 20th Century Fox in 1940. I was watching her film a new movie as I sat on the lap of Janet Gaynor, a star from a previous generation. My parents were very excited about meeting Janet Gaynor. I had never heard of her before, but I did know who Shirley Temple was – well sort of. Janet Gaynor was the first actress to win an academy award in 1939, for her starring role in the movie, *Seventh Heaven*. She co-starred with Charles Farrell.

I watched Shirley Temple perform before lights and cameras and lots of people. They treated her like a princess. My child size, four-year-old ego kicked right in and I do remember saying, "I want to be up there doing what she is doing." At that point, I had one year of ballet "under my feet" and had starred in a ballet production. I was ready. To my great disappointment we left the studio never to return.

I saw Shirley Temple once again, years later at I. Magnin in Stanford Shopping Center, California. At that time, I was with my seven-year-old daughter. Thanks to reruns on TV, my daughter did know who she was.

Shirley Temple had left Hollywood far behind, just as I had many years earlier.

GEORGE CHRISTOPHER

George Christopher was the mayor of San Francisco from 1956 to 1964. He had the redoubtable honor of being the last Republican to hold that office to date.

He was also Greek, which is why I met him when I attended a Greek wedding reception in 1962. I went with a friend of mine who was Greek.

George Christopher was an affable and practiced politician, and in that atmosphere, among friends, very much at ease.

That particular wedding reception remains distinct in my mind of all the wedding receptions I have attended through the years.

Why? Yes, dance and sing and *break dishes*. Smash, smash, smash—kind of fun – actually. And there was the mayor smashing with glee with the rest of us. I did find out that cheap dishes were used—not the good china. It was great fun.

SALLY STANFORD

A celebrity in every sense of the word—famous *and* notorious.

She was a former celebrated madam in San Francisco for years, an author of "A House is Not a Home," the owner of the once famous Valhalla Restaurant in Sausalito, and a mayor of Sausalito, California.

Many people went to her restaurant in Sausalito to see her more than to dine. I do not know if she was usually there but she was there when I drove over the Golden Gate Bridge with a girlfriend, so we could check it out.

We were halfway through dinner when she "sallied" over to our table, with her trademark on her shoulder, her parrot, and began to talk with us. Somehow, we got the uneasy feeling, being in our early twenties, the way she looked us over that she was "interviewing" us for a "Job"?

We were happy and somewhat relieved to leave and never return.

JANET LEIGH & TONY CURTIS

They were Hollywood royalty in the 1950's and the powers that be in Hollywood did an outstanding job of packaging and marketing them as such. They were continually on display wherever they went. In public, they were more of a commodity than a couple and a very profitable and lucrative one.

Unfortunately, human beings, being what we are—human—cannot withstand the constant demands that such a far-from-natural and from-the-moon and-back lifestyle brings to bear on a relationship and on each person individually.

I was with my family, dining at the Coconut Grove (Ambassador Hotel) in Los Angeles, CA in the 1950's when their fame and celebrity was at its all-time high. Our table was right next to theirs. They were beautiful, glamorous and the focus and center of attention of everyone in the room.

What pressure!

At least people respected their privacy, except for the gawking; no one spoke to them all evening except the waiters.

It was a thrill dining so near to them. I had a huge fourteen-year-old crush on these two super stars of Hollywood at that time.

I saw Janet Leigh a few years later at the Racquet Club in Palm Springs when she was going through a separation and divorce. She was sitting at a table in the lounge and the tears were flowing. It was tragic to see one so lovely in so much pain.

ROWAN & MARTIN

Rowan and Martin performed at a convention held at the Palace Hotel in 1962.

I was working for a firm in San Francisco as an executive secretary and fortunately, for me, my boss was not dating anyone at the time.

Since he was one of the principals of the event he needed a date to join him at the head table along with several other couples. There were several hundred people who would be attending.

Rowan and Martin doing their stand-up act.

One morning he said he wanted to see me in his office at noon. Of course, my first thought was, I must be in trouble for something. Unless I was taking dictation (the days of shorthand and notepads and typewriters) he never asked me into his office at lunchtime.

I arrived at noon, knocked and entered his office I was met with a friendly smile and a setup of lunch for two.

I was surprised to say the least, and thought, *"What's up with this?"*

Soon my question was answered when halfway through lunch he asked, "Would you like to be my date at the convention?"

After I recovered from the shock, of course, I said, "Yes, that would be great."

Rowan and Martin performed that evening and they had the audience in an uproar of laughter the whole time. They were a gifted, talented, brilliant, and a fairly unknown comedy team. They had been playing in nightclubs around the United States and overseas for years.

After their routine was finished they came over and joined us at our table and related some of their experiences of traveling around the country with their act.

One of the men at our table told them, "You guys are terrific. More people should know about you."

That did happen a few years later, in 1968, when they introduced Laugh-In to the world and for them, international fame and fortune.

They had paid their "dues."

ADOLPH SPRECKLES, MOLOTOV & GROMYKO

Adolph Spreckles Jr., the heir to the Spreckles Sugar fortune, lived in the estate behind my parents in Hillsborough, California. Actually, his estate was behind the vacant lot my parents had purchased as an investment and also a protection against any house being built next to their estate.

Adolph also visited Palm Springs from time to time, staying at Ingleside Inn. So we knew him from there as well. He was about the age of my grandfather and whenever my grandfather came down from Victoria (Vancouver Island) BC, Canada, to visit they would pal around.

Vyacheslav Molotov

But that is not quite the end of the reminiscence.

One day the Russians (Soviets) arrived.

Now, at that time, the Cold War was beginning to get more intense, so it was quite an intimidating prospect and a bit scary to have them living next door.

Adolph Spreckles had rented his home to the Soviet delegation that was attending the Peace Treaty of San Francisco Conference in September 1951.

Two of my girlfriends and I decided that we would walk over to the empty lot to investigate after they had arrived.

We could see the back of the Spreckles house, the pool, patio, and umbrella tables clearly from the vacant lot.

The first day we did not see much of anything. But the second afternoon we saw Molotov and Gromyko sitting at an umbrella table by the pool.

It was about that time that we developed plans for the next afternoon. When we got home from school we met at the empty lot where we once again saw these two men sitting around the pool. We each gathered shovels with which we proceeded to dig a mock grave, representing the thousands who had died and were dying in the Siberian slave camps. We continued to dig for a while as we sang "The Song of the Volga Boatmen" as loud as we could so Molotov and Gromyko could hear us.

After a while, we left, planning on returning the next day, which we did...with our shovels. We began our second performance, though indeed, not at all by popular demand. It was not long before Gromyko came over onto our property (he was trespassing actually) with four burly men we suspected were KGB agents. I guess three fourteen-year-old teenage girls posed a "threat" of some kind.

He approached us as the KGB stood a few feet behind him. He did not seem too happy.

He did not introduce himself either, but immediately began to interrogate us.

"Do you speak Russian?" he asked.

"No," we replied.

He continued, "Do you speak Chinese?"

"No," we answered.

Then my friend, Judy, piped up and said, "But I speak Spanish."

He gave us a look of disgust, turned around and left.

The next day United States and international newsmen arrived and asked if they could take pictures from the empty lot which afforded them a total view of the house, upstairs and downstairs, and the pool area. We could always see people walking around in the house and I am sure with their telephoto lenses they could see who was inside.

Of course, we invited all of them from all over the world onto the property. They were elated. There were more than a dozen of them, and, of course, it was thrilling for the three of us to meet them and talk to all of them . . . well, those we could understand, actually, the ones who spoke English but the rest were happy and smiling . . . and no wonder . . .What others had those pictures? I am sure their editors gave them all bonuses.

Several days later, when we went over again after school, the reporters and photographers began arriving. Only this time the scene had changed.

Molotov and Gromyko no longer came outside and all of the drapes were drawn on the upper and lower floors.

Naturally, we never informed our parents of this incident.

NELSON ROCKEFELLER

I met him in the early 1960's at the Alta Mira Hotel in Sausalito, California.

Working in San Francisco as an executive secretary at that time, this bit of trivia is a departure from the encounters of my younger years.

A friend, who also worked in the city, and I decided to celebrate the end of the workweek with a special treat. We drove across the Golden Gate Bridge to Sausalito to dine in the Alta Mira hotel dining room. The food at the time was excellent and the view superb.

As we were finishing our dessert and coffee our waiter came up to our table with the information that Nelson

Nelson Rockefeller, as Governor of New York.

Rockefeller had just arrived for an informal reception. He said that if we were interested, he could sneak us into the room and to the back of the reception line. We did not have to think twice, "Sure", was our answer. We looked around the room from the back of the reception line of about forty people. Everyone was a lot older; we were in our early twenties. Most of the guests were in their fifties and sixties.

The women wore expensive cocktail dresses and some pretty impressive jewelry; the men were dressed in suits and ties. We were wearing sweaters and skirts.

Fortunately, since we were standing at the back of the line, no one noticed us. I do not think we would have made it to the front of the room otherwise. Everyone was looking forward, as the line moved toward Rockefeller.

The line moved slowly. It seemed everyone had a lot to say to him. Finally, after about thirty minutes, we were standing directly in front of him.

I remember so clearly what he said to us while shaking our hands: "Young ladies, what are *you* doing here?" Actually, we didn't have an answer. His charisma, charm, and good looks were kind of overwhelming, and we were a bit tongue-tied.

Anyway, without any effort, he picked up the slack and made us feel welcome and comfortable. I do not remember what else was said, but on the way driving back to San Francisco we decided, with the wisdom of twenty-something year-olds, that he was the type of person one could invite to dinner and serve hot dogs and he would be just fine with it.

JULIA CHILD

I met Julia at a gathering of about 25 women at the San Francisco Yacht Club in the1960's. About twenty women attended her talk and cooking class.

It was an interesting couple of hours. The impact and vitality of her personality dominated the gathering. She was positive, humorous, as one would gather from her first and popular TV show, based on her best-selling book, *Mastering the Art of French Cooking.* She loved to cook and to pass on her knowledge and expertise.

I do not remember what we learned that day, I am sure it was useful. I did come away with an autographed copy of her first edition which I am sure is worth a lot of money to someone today, unfortunately, not to me. Not that I would want to sell it. But years ago, someone did "lift" it from my house, never to be seen again.

A few years after that gathering a friend, who flew for an airline, route – east coast to west coast, arrived with 4 live lobsters. I had never looked a live lobster in the eye before and I must say, I was hugely intimidated.

I do not remember if I thanked him as he left. I felt conflicted about this "gift."

By then Julia's book had disappeared and I had not replaced it. I still have not to this day. Somehow it would not be the same.

Anyway, left to my own devices and wishing Julia would ring the doorbell at any minute, I gathered up my courage and began to address the cooking of the lobsters for guests that evening.

First boil water. I put in some "stuff" for flavoring.

Next open the box of lobsters.

This is when I ran (literally) into trouble.

One of the lobsters jumped out – *at me* – and onto the kitchen floor.

I fled the kitchen, screaming.

A few minutes later I peeked around the kitchen door and saw it was still lying there. It was then that I noticed that its claws were pegged. So, no worries. By then the water was boiling. I got the longest tongs I could find and lifted them one-by-one into the boiling water and quickly put on the lid.

Then I had what I will call "Chef's Remorse." It is a stretch to call myself a chef but I thought what the heck, I went to Julia's workshop, so why not.

Anyway, I was waiting to hear them scream. All was silent. Then I wondered if they felt any pain. "Did they suffer?" I asked myself. After considering those possibilities I felt like crying. Actually, I have decided that I am just a cook, plain and simple, for I do not think a *real* chef would have had those reactions.

Suffice to say, those were the first and the last live lobsters I prepared.

EPILOGUE

Some of us walk down the street and nobody knows us.

Some of us walk down the street and soon we are mobbed by fans.

Some of us are content.

Some of us long for money, fame, power.

Almost all of us want more.

More ice cream, more sun, more rain, more friends, more love, more adventure, more freedom, more vacations, more – more – more.

How often do we yearn for less?

Less happiness, less fun, less sleep, less ability, less joy, less peace, less beauty, *and* less ice cream? Almost never.

What does any of this have to do with traveling through?

It is the essence of it.

More or Less!

Other Books by Jeanne Beatty

Coming Soon

The Empty Pillow

Wrinkled Lips
101 Gifts From Grandmothers

Standing on the Rock

Stolen Tomorrows

Landscapes

Made in the USA
Las Vegas, NV
26 September 2021